Radical PI

Personal Invent

Joe Caulfield

And

Rodney Diekema

This book is licensed for your personal enjoyment. It may not be resold or given away. If you would like to share this book, please purchase an additional copy for each person with whom you want to share it. If you're reading this book and did not purchase it, or if it was not purchased for your use only, please purchase your own copy. Thank you for respecting the authors' work.

Radical PEO Sales Success™ and *Personal Inventory Assessment Selling*™ is a registered trademark by the United States Patent Office.

ACKNOWLEDGMENTS

Thank you Malcolm Gladwell (Blink), Dan Kennedy, Garry Duncan (Leadership Connections), Dale Carnegie, the American Management Association, Virginia Satir, and Richard Bandler and John Grinder (Frogs into Princes), Steve Jobs, Maxwell Maltz (Psycho-Cybernetics), Earl Nightingale, Zig Ziglar, Tony Robbins, Napoleon Hill and others.

It is my hope that this book helps YOU to take creative control of your success in PEO sales consulting or management.

From Steve Jobs:
"Here's to the crazy ones, the misfits, rebels, trouble makers, round pegs in square holes, ones who see things differently. They are not fond of rules, they have no respect for status quo, you can quote them, you can disagree with them, glorify them or vilify them but the only thing you can't do is ignore them because they change things, they push the human race forward." ~ Steve Jobs

From Dan Kennedy:

"In this economy, it's more important than ever to do things differently. Business as usual has gotten us into one of the biggest economic messes we've seen in decades.

It wasn't your fault. But if you don't keep your head on a swivel, constantly surveying the horizon for ways to be different, you'll wind up as just another bleached carcass in the desert. Business as usual means failure. Especially in this Economy." ~ Dan Kennedy

INTRODUCTION

"He that will not apply new remedies must expect new evils; for time is the greatest innovator." ~Francis Bacon

Normal versus Radical

It's very easy to get stuck in the way we do things—it is our *normal*. We hit the office at a certain time, check email, and then hit the telephone, or we go to that early networking breakfast, and while on the way check out our iPhone/ Android/iPad for any urgent items, which includes Twitter, Facebook and Linkedin, then we go to our office, handle whatever needs handling, and then hit the phones, emails or direct mail to generate appointments. It seems like half or more of our life is involved in getting the appointment. We have, over time honed our skills on handling the phone and networking events to maximize our chances to GET that appointment. Once on a face-to-face sales call, we begin with what has become our own individualized method of presenting to a potential business owner, which we have found leads us to the first major goal—A Request For Proposal. Once that is accomplished, 50% of time if we are really good, our activity resembles that of a fluttering bird in a stiff breeze. We know we have to collect relevant data at hyper-speed, or we lose any chance of a successful final outcome of a new client.

Then, if the gods, karma, and mojo are with us, which can include various underwriting departments, sales bosses, and IF the pricing is good enough to glean a profit in that first twelve months of a new client; we have a deal.

Whoops, not done yet, because now your work shifts to orientation and client services, which, mostly, is a lot of exacting, I mean exciting paperwork regarding medical and payroll. Hopefully, in your company, you have some help with this. Plus there is now the caveat of explaining to your new client that all things new create at least a little confusion, and that they need to communicate to you what is happening at their end, directly to you. In other words, the new client needs a baby-sitter for the first few payrolls, or until they build a relationship with your company client service professionals and payroll department.

All the aforementioned are when that face-to-face sales call goes right. How often is it going right for you? In most statistical models, the best possible is 50% of those first sales calls leading to a Request For Proposal, and 20% move to a sale. This percentage is also someone with full training and lots of experience. New people typically are below 25%. This is what could be called a "Normal" sales cycle for new and experienced PEO sales consultants. Is it enough?

If it's not, then something **radical**, yet proven, could be attempted; radical in the sense that it is out of our normal behavior patterns — away from that *"Business as usual"* that Dan Kennedy talks about. Something different must be really revolutionary for it to boost you to a new level.

Everything you want, everything you have and everything you are about to do somehow, someway, involves "selling." (1)

Are you satisfied with your sales life, or is there a need for improvement? There is an old saying that if you keep doing what you are doing, then you're going to keep getting what you're getting. Is it enough?

Dan Kennedy has also stated, "I think rules are there for ordinary mortals — certainly not for me, and not for you either if you are a true entrepreneur. So you'll chafe at rules here just as I would. However, when you are attempting to un-do bad habits and replace them with new ones, some hard and fast rules are necessary, temporarily.

Once you fully understand those and have lived with them for a reasonable length of time, then feel free to experiment if you wish. But get good at coloring inside the lines before ignoring them altogether." (16)

In starting my company *Rapid* Sales Success, I began the process of putting the finishing touches on a *Personal Inventory Assessment Selling* process that provided the opportunity to more closely manage the PEO sale — to help everyone on both sides of the sales aisle reach their goals. Methodological processes have the advantage of knowing exactly where you're succeeding and where you need improvement; it jumps out at you. This type of process keeps sales consultants, and prospects focused and on track.

It's been said you can't effectively manage what you can't measure. The Radical PEO Sales technique will help you measure your success each step of the way, and puts you in control.

PEO Consultants are successful to the degree that we can positively influence the prospect's mental buying habits and change behaviors, which result in an informed decision.

Where Should Your Head Be?

The mentality that has been successful for many PEO sales consultants is to adopt the attitude that you're running your own business, never allowing your loyalty to your PEO Company to be alloyed. This puts you in command of: sales, marketing, social marketing, orientations, and customer service. I could go on, but you get the idea. (See Chapter Twenty.)

Mentally, you are on your own, and you can eat what you catch. Your company becomes a valuable resource that can help you. They provide you all the necessities like a place to sit, telephone, training, advice and opinion, brochures, forms, advertising, and do all of that pesky (not) vendor work that needs constant attention with health insurance, workers' comp, legal, and other value-added pieces, which provide you a sellable product, and all of this at no cost to you.

This somewhat small shift in my thinking made me think about what I'd do if I were the PEO owner, right now. Would I go to that networking event at 6:00 AM? How about doing that direct mail campaign? Would I make that extra cold call?

The answer routinely came back as a yes. It made me work harder and more responsibly.

PRELUDE

"I Just Need Business."

"I need a PEO salesperson who can sell."

"Give me a few good salespeople, and I will light the world on fire."

"Salespeople are liars."

"Salespeople's paperwork is a joke."

"That salesperson couldn't sell their way out of a paper bag."

These are the kind of statements I've heard for years from PEO owners, and sales manager; they are right.

I watched, as good to great people could not make the grade in selling PEO. I saw managers, and owners become frustrated by the lack of activity and the lack of results, even though their hiring systems were good. If you don't hire properly no sales system or process in the world is going to produce good results. I listened as they said, "There has to be a better way."

I was really driven to succeed. Hell, I was a single dad with two kids, and so I made it my mission to discover what was going on, for my own success and survival.

I examined the people first. Were PEOs simply not hiring the right people, not on-boarding correctly, not training adequately, or paying too low? Was it the right person, but the wrong industry? The answers were mostly a resounding, "No," in most cases.

What was the problem that kept stopping PEOs and the people they hired from achieving their ideal, on a consistent basis? And, what was the solution?

I felt comfortable that it wasn't the different sales process systems, because I tried everything from PSS (Professional Selling Skills) (23) to the old Attention, Interest, Conviction, Desire and Close, where if you got an objection, then you answered it and CLOSED again — right away.

The good news is that all of those systems work. The bad news is they did not work well enough.

What?

That's right! When done *purely*, they worked — to a degree. It was that 'to a degree' part that bothered me. The reward never seemed to keep pace with my tremendous efforts.

Within any sales team that I've ever been associated with—over all, the processes did not work for most. Was I some kind of super salesman? Hardly, since I struggled like everyone else. Nevertheless, I always managed to stay _near_ the top of the leader board. Why? That became the big question. Also, why wasn't my name routinely at the very top of the leader board?

In my past life with an orthopedic implant company (Howmedica), I had a trainee of mine, Miles Cannon, tell me one day that I had a knack for noticing the obvious. At the time, I was unsure whether that was an insult or a compliment, but the statement did encourage me to take a look.

Eventually, I ran upon the term Occam's Razor, which states that the simpler of two competing theories is the one to be preferred—it is the process of paring down information to make finding the truth easier. It is getting rid of all the assumptions that make no difference to the predictions of a hypothesis. As you can see—there's that knack for noticing the obvious.

As I studied the problem, of "I want more sales—I don't want more sales," I grew more and more confused, as everything seemed to work—<u>to a degree</u>.

Was I just going to put up with that *to a degree* part? I admit it—I languished.

Then, someone said that anytime you introduced order, you are guaranteed to get confusion. The thing to do according to the seminar leader was to keep introducing the order and the confusion would eventually go away. I continued introducing order—it worked. (1)

Well, where was that knack for noticing the obvious? I looked at everything within the sales process a.k.a. lead conversion, to such a minute degree that I was going balmy. Satisfying, results producing answers was simply not there; at least, I could not see it.

So, I moved to an entire system overview of the overall sales/marketing process.

Here are the typical steps: (2)
    1. Generate Leads = Marketing

2. Qualify = Marketing and Sales

3. Lead Conversion = Sales

It stands to reason that if PEOs could generate leads and then qualify the prospect, we sales consultants could, through almost any sales process bring in revenue. The good news is that it works. The bad news; it is with drab percentages. Yes, breakout moments occur, and we call those people heroes. That does little to handle the entire sales group though. *(Later, I studied the 'heroes')*

Perhaps it was just a matter of seeing more prospects — more activity, hitting the phones harder, sending out more letters or emails, more social and other networking? In fact, this is the answer most PEO's adopt as a solution because they don't know what to do instead. Well, that does work, but burn out and turnover in most companies is also atrocious — and very costly. The closing percentage is equally dismal.

The current PEO sales system was killing off the salespeople by burning them out — making them lose. In talking with others, I found that a lot of people believe that maybe that is just the way it is. It is just a tough damn industry.

"Wait a minute," I thought in bewilderment, as I listened to myself, *"the system is killing off the salespeople. Let's take a closer look at the entire system, and let's start with step number one – Generate Leads."*

It could not have been more tedious. This book only gives the results that worked, not all of that research. Thank goodness, right? Plus, many of the component parts were released as found, so some of the tools have been out there, but without the entire process, the level of success is minimal — watered downed.

I have had a call recently (2012) from a sales administrator from a huge PEO that claimed his company had developed one of the Radical Sales Success tools that was part of that 'tedious' time. I laughed, and said, "Okay, when did you guys develop this?" He said, "2005." I sent him a proof copy of the developed piece dated 2001. When I called to discuss it, he was not available.

I should let you know that just having PEO sales tools does little good without the training that goes with it. Sales consultants just won't use it. It is like buying an exercise machine and then thinking just by owning it, or looking at it you'll lose weight. It turns out that perfect practice makes perfect.

The steps of the *total* Radical PEO Sales system are:

Define a Perfect/Ideal Client

Survey the Perfect Client's Buying Habits

Do Psychographic survey on client base

Conduct a Pareto Analysis of Critical Success Factors from sales

Develop a Commonality of Issues Sheet (Personal Inventory Assessment list — a.k.a. CIS)

Install the Process

Market to the Perfect Client — Generate Leads

Qualification of the Prospect — do they match the profile

Face-to-Face Calls

If you are a PEO executive, here is some great news you should know. Recent surveys tell us that the major reason that sales training does not work is because there is a lack of buy-in, at the top of the organizational chart. This, unfortunately, translates into a lack of discipline of the entire sales team. This lack of discipline includes sales management, in making sure any new system and process is duplicated and *done*. The result is no changes in sales behaviors. It makes sales training look as though it did not work.

Your sales group collectively drags their feet until the next big deal training thing comes around, or until management reads — the newest book. As a result, very little ever changes. A program must be found that works and then stick to it. Now that this is known, it can be worked on, and fixed. Any new sales system would have to be a lot different from your 'normal' in order to get different results.

There are two distinctly different parts of Radical PEO Sales Success. The first is the pre-work (structural pieces); the second is the actual sales process itself.

The pre-work is:

Define a Perfect Client

Survey the Perfect Client's Buying Reasons

Do Psychographic surveys

Conduct a Pareto analysis of Critical Success Factors for Sales

Develop a Commonality of Issues Sheet (Personal Inventory Assessment list/CIS)

The Radical PEO Sales process represents a paradigm shift. It transforms the normal, somewhat *boring* informational presentation type sales system into a *Personal Inventory Assessment* sales consultancy.

Why boring? Most current prospects *think* they are familiar with our industry when we show up. They've been on the Internet and know some of the nuts and bolts. They may have listened to a digital/virtual presentation, or seen a slideshow on PEO. This is a little like reading a book on neurosurgery and thinking you are now a surgeon.

In today's world, the informational type of presentation never quite gets to the meat of the problems that the prospect personally wants solved. We pretend to know, but we've forgotten to ask.

This is because that informational presentation expects the prospect to connect the dots and solve it internally. Unfortunately, this does not happen often enough. Thus, we have low percentage closing ratios.

What PEO sales consultants end up doing is what I call "shotgunning" by bringing up everything a PEO can do for a client all at once. We hope, and sometimes pray that something will click or stick with the prospect. This Radical PEO Sale system is close to the exact opposite of shotgunning.

Here, we are doing a *Personal Inventory Assessment to determine what the prospect actually wants us to solve, according to them.*

This Radical PEO Sales process is a consultant method that personally interacts through simple questioning in discovering a prospect's thinking contained within any buying incidences that were similar in the prospect's purchasing history. It then provides the prospect with self-evident solutions. I know. It sounds complex, but instead it is way simple.

Through the utilization of: (The boring necessary parts)
Demographics

Psychographic surveys

Analysis

Perfect client profiles

Client surveys

Face-to-face calls to track Critical Success Factors

Presented here is the process that takes advantage of street-wise technologies. *This resulted in a simple, but extremely consultative, high-impact, yet high touch PEO process – that works.*

It represents the shift from a somewhat mechanical model to an empathetic, customer-centric model. ***It raises closing ratios***.

Let's do something unusual (radical) here, and skip to the ending – so you can get a look at a first call on a prospect that has been analyzed and otherwise scrutinized, utilizing the Personal Inventory Assessment process.

In the example, we know that the person we are calling on is a true prospect, and has been measured against our Perfect Client Profile, marketed to, and have raised their hand. Our paper consultant (me) knows everything I do – this should be good.

This is close to how it works under live fire, in the field.

(This example gives you the **psychographics** of the small-business owner, as well)

Here is Chapter One...

CHAPTER ONE: From Confusion to Clarity

Let's say…

Let's say that average business owners work from 60-80 hours per week. Their schedules are horrendous. They are generally Type-A personality. Right now, they have a lot of worry over the economy, lines of credit, slumping sales, and health care, on top of those usual day-to-day situations.

They are typically married, have children, and know that their business is what supports all of that, plus their somewhat lavish lifestyle, e.g., house, cars, nanny (part-time), vacations, a boat, a summer property, camp for the kids, clothing.

For visualization purposes let's say that a person's mind is similar to a computer, iPhone, iPad or Android, and has only 100 mental attention units, kind of like RAM (random-access memory) of availability to think, compare and comprehend.

Now, let's imagine that this prospect has 60% of those mental attention units on his work (lots of issues — kind of normal), 6% on being tired and/or hungry, and 14% on a sick youngster at home, and an additional 5% on making a 6:00 P.M. meeting, and being prepared. Mentally he is 85% occupied.

And now you, as a PEO *salesperson*, walk through his door for your 4:00 P.M. initial call. This, theoretically, gives you a 15% person to talk with, and you haven't even said hello.

If you launch into a usual getting to know you rapport thing, which is generally a tell me about that (picture on your wall) line, and then a quick, yet professional presentation highlighting the features, benefits and incentives of your company and its products, flashing a brochure or showing a PowerPoint presentation filled with acronyms and perhaps words that our business owner prospect does not understand — well, then, you are relying on two things only.

Number one, the prospect's good grace and manners in just not falling to sleep, or worse — engaging themselves in what I call objection mode — just to stay awake, or, **Number two**, he knows about your industry and was hoping you'd show up — (pre-sold).

Let's say you have the same circumstance, but you walk in with a Radical PEO Sales process as a PEO *consultant, not a salesperson.*

You introduce yourself and establish some rapport as a peer, hopefully, about the thing he really loves — his business — and the next thing he knows you are sitting there making a drawing of some principle called Human Resource Outsourcing (Overview) — *what is that an umbrella?*

Our Human
Resources, Inc.

Human
Resources &
Benefits

Payroll &
Workers
Compensation

Your Administrative
& Human Resource
Departments

(This prospect is forced into the present by this action of engagement.) He thinks, *"Oh yeah, there's the umbrella handle and labels on each side of the handle — human resources, benefits and then payroll and worker's comp — hmm-so what — at least it's interesting — different"*.

Then he hears you say, "Most CEOs have some kind of commonality of issues", and the consultant shoves this form toward you; the Commonality of Issues Sheet-CIS-*Personal Inventory Assessment*, and says something about — "if I am wasting your time, I'll leave" — *(sounds good) — what's he talking about anyway?*

Oh yeah, human resources, benefits and jeez, workers' compensation stuff. Good Lord, he wants me to take a test. Oh well, let me at least look at it. It is short.

Hmm! (Prospect's looking at CIS sheet) *we do need some improvement on this one, and this one too, what the heck, I guess it can't hurt to fill it out.* He gives you the Commonality of Issues Sheet (CIS) back.

Now you, <u>*the consultant*</u>, take each question that he checked off as "needs improvement", you do the Rapid Recall System, giving a proper acknowledgement after each answer — having <u>empathy</u>. (Take copious notes here)

(Here is how the Rapid Recall System works)

You say, "Worker's Compensation" rates are going up?"

He says, "Yes they are…"

You say, "Ouch! Tell me about that."

He does.

Then you acknowledge what he just said and ask, "When was that?"

Prospect answers and you acknowledge. "Okay." Then, "What did _that_ cost you?"

Prospect answers and you ask, after a low whistle. "How did that affect your business?"

Prospect answers and you acknowledge and say, "And, how did that affect you personally?"

Prospect answers and you give an appropriate acknowledgement and ask, "What impact did that have?"

Prospect answers and you once again acknowledge his answer, and then say, "Okay, on a scale from one to ten how committed are you to making sure it never happens again?"

I absolutely promise you, this Prospect is not going to fall to sleep or start in with any kind of 'Objection Mode' game — he is fully engaged.

He is engaged because he is communicating on something that's important to him — his concerns, his worries, his business, his lifestyle, his wife, his kids, his boat. Please note also, HE is communicating. You are merely asking questions. (10) You would repeat this process on every hot button item that turns up on our **short** *Personal Inventory Assessment* (CIS).

Let's say however, that this prospect has the opposite reaction and will not even look at your beautifully drawn umbrella, and will not fill out the Commonality of Issues Sheet. What should you do? Leave. Yes, leave. Do it nicely, but get out of there.

Why? Look, all kinds of your company's current clients that were eventually called "Perfect/Ideal Clients" because they were so nice to work with ended up helping to formulate the Perfect Client Profile Club, and this prospect just voted himself out of that exclusive club.

He self-deselected. Next.

There could be a bunch of reasons he wouldn't play and quite honestly it's not important — we are not clinical psychologist; we are PEO sales consultant psychologists — a huge difference. He, by his inaction, has shown a lack of harmony with the psychographic profile.

Trust the system.

He just saved you from wasting a lot of your *time*, effort, and energy, and lots of company money.

Okay, if you insist, put him on a drip marketing campaign and call him once more after a few weeks if you like.

Well, what did you think?

Following is the rest of the story.

CHAPTER TWO: Empathy and Thought Software

In Radical PEO Sales, *empathy* has similarities in sales consultant psychology to *sympathy*, but the viewpoints are entirely separate, and very distinct. Both words imply an attempt toward understanding and the entering into another's feelings. Sympathy however, has what could be called a point of actual agreement and rapport with those feelings, whereas with empathy you are able to remain apart from and objective, as the solver of problems.

For our purposes therefore, empathy is good and sympathy is bad in a PEO sales consultant call.

This book gives the tools you need to be a more effective PEO consultant by enhancing some skills you already possess. Some of that new enhancement has to do with words, and word usage. You see, in the top echelons of consultative selling, there is an extreme awareness of words — the nomenclature used in the art of consulting.

You can't persuade people, or give advice if you don't speak their language. Furthermore, you can't speak their language unless you develop a heightened awareness of whether your communication is being understood.

Sales Consultants should be hyper-vigilant in guarding against using words or acronyms that a potential client does not understand. (9) Why?

The human mind cannot process what it does not understand.

An undefined word or acronym given to a prospect's search engine (the mind-think Internet search) can have the effect of severely slowing or even shutting down their own *thought-software*.

Computers were slowly developed with the help of cybernetics. Cybernetics is the field of science concerned with processes of communication and control, especially the comparison of these processes in biological and artificial systems.

This is to say; human thinking was studied to create the computer.

Undefined words or symbols act like a thought software *virus*, and have the effect that your prospect will get bored, sleepy, defensive, antagonistic and/or withdrawn (similar to your computer). This is not what we want.

Therefore, it becomes *imperative* that we not introduce this thought software virus to our prospects. Using undefined words on sales call is counter-productive. Use those old nickel words, or define things as you go along. Do not assume that your prospect understands Family Medical Leave Act, when you say, FMLA, or ACA; say Affordable Care Act.

In keeping with the spirit of the above, I have included a glossary in the back of this book that contains some definitions taken from dictionaries, my own experiences, and other miscellaneous sources that will be used throughout the book.

CHAPTER THREE: Persuasion Architecture

The following pages map out a blueprint of persuasion architecture based upon what the prospect wants, instead of what we think or even know what they need.

The demographics of the PEO industry are complete, the psychographics have been compiled, and the analysis has been formulated based on perfect client surveys expressing "wants" _at the time of purchasing PEO_. The rule is:

Sell them what they want — deliver what they want and need.

As you read, there are two things occurring. One is structure, and the other is process. The _Personal Inventory Assessment_ approach of PEO selling refers to a _systematic process of repetitive and measurable milestones, by which a sales consultant relates the offering of a product or service._

We now get to dig into a term you have probably heard since birth – The 80-20 Rule.

CHAPTER FOUR: Historical Background: The 80-20 Rule/Pareto Analysis

<u>Major Player</u>

Obituary: Joseph Moses Juran (December 24, 1904 – February 28, 2008) Helped establish the field of quality management and wrote the "Quality Control Handbook," which taught manufacturers worldwide how to be more efficient and productive, died Thursday in Rye, N.Y., where he lived with his wife of 81 years, Sadie. He was 103. He created the Pareto Principle, also known as the "80-20 Rule", which states that 80 percent of consequences stem from 20 percent of the causes. Today managers use the Pareto Principle, named for an Italian economist, to help them separate what Mr. Juran called the "vital few" resources from the "useful many." (14)
By NICK BUNKLEY, March 3, 2008

A Pareto Analysis can be effectively employed in order to separate the major causes (the "Vital Few") of successes, from the minor ones (the "Useful Many").

Such an analysis focuses attention to tackling the major causes of success at hand, rather than wasting valuable time on the minor ones — the "useful (or trivial) many".

Application of the 80-20 Rule in business

The Pareto Principle (80-20 Rule) proves itself in practically every area of management — some of which are:

20 percent of the customers account for 80 percent of the sales.

20 percent of the products or services account for 80 percent of the profits.

20 percent of your inventory takes up 80 percent of your warehouse space.

20 percent of your suppliers provide 80 percent of your inventory

20 percent of your sales force will provide 80 percent of your sales.

20 percent of your staff will cause 80 percent of your problems.

20 percent of a company's staff will output 80 percent of its production.

20 percent of people who have failed due to miscommunication did so because

80 percent of the time they neglected to clear up misunderstood words.

The 80-20 Rule appears to be a universal truth that applies to practically all aspects of management and even to one's personal life.

The analysis has been proven to be a powerful and effective tool for making continuous improvement and for problem solving. Many have discovered that continued application of the 80-20 Rule in sales greatly improves productivity, quality, and profitability.

As mentioned, the principle of Pareto's Law was suggested and expanded by management guru Joseph Juran (1941). It was named after the Italian economist Vilfredo Pareto. The value of the Pareto Principle for sales management is that it is a reminder to focus on the 20 percent that create Critical Success Factors (CSF) (5).

The analysis is a <u>statistical</u> technique in decision-making that is used for selecting a limited number of tasks that can produce the most substantial and significant overall effect. The analysis is a technique useful where many possible courses of action are competing for attention.

In essence, an analysis of each action is done. Then you select, based on desired results, the number of the most effective actions that deliver a total benefit, reasonably close to the ideal results.

These effective actions are put onto a bar chart where the values plotted are arranged in a descending order. Imbedded within the bar graph is a line graph that shows the totals of each category. Other charts include cause & effect and flowchart.

In other words, we are taking a course of action that accomplishes the most, with minimal use of resources.

<u>80% of results come from 20% of activities.</u>

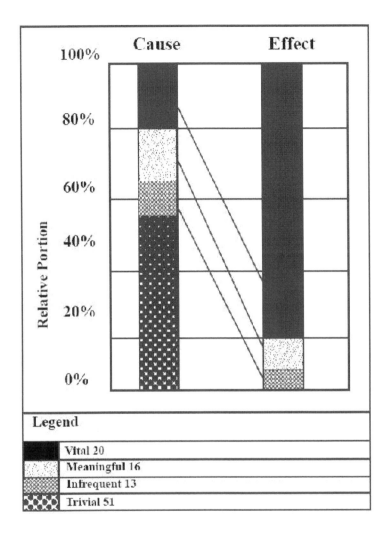

In the diagram, the column on the left is the "Cause" column for the situation that we are studying, and the column on the right is the "Effect" column. It is clear that one is either *cause* or *effect*. This is one way we tracked the 'vital few'. Results.

"The problem that arises in selling is when you're attempting to be, "the cause" and instead finds s/he is trapped into being part of "the effect."

Other situations arise when not enough data is present. As an example, a man may have high blood pressure and wrongfully view that the cause was not taking his medication.

However, if he figuratively peeled the onion in order to get to the root cause of the problem (more data), he would discover that the real cause of his high blood pressure is the result of a poor diet and a lack of cardio-vascular exercise.

Individuals and companies sometimes budget for a "pill" for the life of their corporation that merely treats a symptom, looking for that simple, expedient solution. Many ill-advised decisions are made for the sake of expediency, at the expense of long-term growth.

Instead of a pill, the ideal is to be able to correct and assure long-term health by making the proper choices in the context of an ever-changing environment. Pills (short-term expedient solutions) can lose their effectiveness and have undesired and sometimes catastrophic side effects. Adaptability and sharply defining the initial problem is always effective.

Before making a sales call, do your homework, not only on the company you're calling on, but their competitors.

See if you can ascertain, or anticipate emerging industry trends. (It is, oddly, rather easy to do.)

Strategically evaluate where the prospect's company fits in to the total picture. With this data you can be more successful. In addition to selling the PEO value proposition, you will have an idea of where their product or service fits in during their industry's next paradigm shift. Your prospect will see that you've done your homework.

Homework can be as simple as a fifteen minute Internet search.

PEO sales professionals should be adept at managing massive amounts of change in order to remain at cause, in an intelligent, timely manner or risk being "at effect."

Being the effect generally equals discomfort.

If markets are changing and we don't, then we'll be forced to make changes on the fly as we attempt to catch up... if we can. Successful consultants I studied rarely waste time and energy trying to play catch-up. Instead, they are continuously and proactively evolving their skill-sets, understanding that change, along with its inherent discomfort (effect), must be carefully introduced in bite-sized pieces, in order to increase market share.

In other words, change should be accomplished on a gradient, a little bit at a time and continuously, not on the fly.

You *must understand* that <u>anytime</u> order is introduced there is a resultant confusion — it is part of a natural process. *If you keep introducing order, the confusion will subside. Do not chase or attempt to handle the confusion, as you will end up with more confusion. Radical PEO Sales is introducing order.*

This book focuses on successful actions only, with no hyperbole, because it has been noted in our quantum world that *when you place attention on what is right, what is incorrect or wrong diminishes or goes away altogether.*

CHAPTER SIX: The PEO Industry

Using Professional Employer Organizations (PEOs) a Pareto's Analysis was done to ascertain the 'Vital Few' critical success factors in selling within our industry. We also worked with, and/or surveyed every top sales consultant we could find — the heroes.

A large sampling of current PEO clients was surveyed in order to determine the psychographics of actual buyers and their reasons for buying. This resulted in the Commonality of Issues Sheet (shown later), which is merely a compilation of their hot buttons — put into a question format. It is also called a *Personal Inventory Assessment*.

By doing small surveys, interviews and analysis, any company or *individual* with a product or service can take advantage of this process.

Background for the newly initiated in PEO

The PEO industry is comprised of companies that sell "Human Resource Outsourcing" as their product/service.

All have the task of selling to the small and medium business market. PEOs sell to business owners, a turnkey system of human resources that includes:

Payroll + Job Costing +

Worker's Compensation +

OSHA Regulation +

Benefits + Ancillary Benefits

Human Resources +

Regulatory Compliance

Thousands of national sales professionals accomplish the selling of these services.

The business owner is the sales target because of the many different areas that are impacted by PEO within their organizational chart. Therefore, the psychographics results came from the small business owners currently utilizing the services of a PEO.

Let me provide a little background information about the PEO industry. Here is an excerpt from the NAPEO (National Association of Professional Employer Organizations) website. (20)

"The PEO relationship involves a contractual allocation and sharing of employer responsibilities between the PEO and the client's company. This shared employment relationship is called co-employment.

As co-employers with their client companies, PEOs contractually assume substantial employer rights, responsibilities, and risk through the establishment and maintenance of an employer relationship with the workers assigned to its clients.

More specifically, a PEO establishes a contractual relationship with its clients whereby the PEO does the following:

Co-employs workers at client locations, and thereby assumes responsibility as an employer for specified purposes of the workers assigned to the client locations.

Reserves a right of direction and control of the employees.

Shares or allocates with the client employer responsibilities in a manner consistent with maintaining the client's responsibility for its product or service.

Pays wages and employment taxes of the employee out of its own accounts.

Reports, collects and deposits employment taxes with state and federal authorities.

Establishes and maintains an employment relationship with its employees that is intended to be long term and not temporary.

Retains a right to hire, reassign and fire the employees. Small businesses outsource to PEOs the complex and often time consuming tasks of administering the payroll, paying employment-related taxes, regulatory compliance, risk management, recruiting, providing health benefits, and securing workers' compensation coverage, plus important ancillary benefits.

According to PEO Network's 2012 survey, there are 983 PEOs operating in the United States and Canada. The industry's gross revenue has grown as PEOs attract more diverse, fast-growing clients, and as the typical salary of the worksite employee increases.

PEOs provide a high value and efficient outsourcing option for businesses from many different industries. The last count I saw was over 312 different SIC codes.

CHAPTER SEVEN: RSS of PEO/Human Resource Outsourcing

Many PEOs only want already trained people. They lack the resources, and sometimes the knowledge base to train. They trust that any newly hired sales person can sell naturally, without a big learning curve.

However, one of the challenges in the PEO industry is maintaining a supply of efficient new sales people to sell its services; alas, PEOs have accepted the concept that product and service knowledge equals sales training.

NOTHING COULD BE FURTHER FROM THE TRUTH.

We are all familiar with beginner's luck. We see it on the baseball diamond, the bowling alley and with board games. We also see it in business, most observably in the sales arena, where an amiable, extroverted personality is said to have a sales personality, or is a people person.

Upon analysis, however, a large number of extremely successful PEO sales people border on being misanthropes, and appear to have a strong analytical, left-brain component. These so-called analytical types generally use a methodological, consultative sales process.

Current estimates to train PEO sales consultants to a point of *stable* productivity range from 6 months to 12 months.

New hires obviously need to understand the foundational aspects and nuances of payroll, human resources, regulatory compliance, benefits and worker's compensation. This however is background/foundational information and *not* sales training. As you will see, there is an actual technology to sales consultancy in conducting interviews with potential clients.

Sales departments are expected to get results rapidly in order to justify their existence within the companies that they serve. Radical PEO Sales can deliver measured and tested results — quickly, without the normal tug-of-war.

If conflict were a normal part of selling that involves emotions it would seem reasonable that we need to learn how to handle the emotions.

"Conflict, by nature, involves emotions and often the emotions are more important than the issue itself. Either way, both must be dealt with and a great way to deal with the emotional and rational side of conflict is to get all the issues out on the table to be discussed in a rational way." ~Cameron Herold, COO, BackPocket (2012)

You should understand that to most mere observers selling is little more than simply talking to people. This is, of course, not true. In fact that type of thinking can stop forward progress in a sales company.

Many years with lots of trial and error have been devoted to perfecting the Radical PEO Sales process, and a thorough study and analysis of why the top 20% of any sales department have 80% of the sales successes. Let's change that right now.

The answer is in your hands. *The methods in this book work — if you do it — by the numbers — and with precision.* It will appear simplistic — it is. Simple works. Ask Einstein.

Explaining the various nuances of what a PEO sells can be complex, and the consultant first needs to understand PEO services (product training), and then the prospective client needs to be brought to an understanding on how it relates to their business and their P&L. (Profit & Loss Statement)

PEO organizations often believe that if successful sales people with proven records of accomplishment are hired from other industries or even the PEO industry, then they will have a fighting chance to increase their company's market share. Oftentimes what we end up with is a polished PEO presenter whose sales performance is dismal.

PEO is a complex sale with many moving parts.

The solution to dismal close ratios has been to have a "closer" who would generally be the sales manager. They typically get involved after the initial presentation. This occurs when we feel we have a hot prospect. It is hoped that the new consultant will observe the closer and learn through repetition and osmosis. Although this arrangement does have some workability, it is inefficient as a PEO grows.

Radical PEO Sales highlights the successful strategies that PEO Peak Performance Specialists (The Heroes) are utilizing. The routine presented takes those successful actions and puts them into a prioritized selling agenda (the methodological approach), so that it can be taught and duplicated by you.

All the reader need do is read it, role-play it, and do it. You should practice at every opportunity, in every first call, every initial presentation in order to have success. You now have a process that delineates the top 20% of successful actions within our industry — what Juran would call "the vital few." (15)

This format for the selling of PEO solutions must be followed *precisely in order for it to work.* If you are imprecise and therefore partially implement it, then the results will be watered-down/diluted. The assumption is that we have a trained person who thoroughly understands the PEO products and services being offered. These steps and the psychology behind each one, done completely, will need a coach/twin to "Read It, Role Play It, Do It" until it is natural and can be delivered conversationally. Team up with someone and practice.

The sale of PEO services is peer-to-peer, not sales person to business *owner* — and, it is consultative and conversational in nature. The psychographics data on PEO clients made it abundantly clear that an overwhelming percentage of business owners dislike sales people. They do however, like consultants.

CHAPTER EIGHT: The PEO Sales Outline

Here is the outline of the approach:

1. Overview
2. Commonality of Issues
3. Rapid Recall System
4. Gathering of Data
5. Custom Presentation Addressing Pain
6. The Cost Box
7. Handling Objections
8. The Close
9. Timeline/Client Calendar
10. Referrals

In the Overview we can either use a PowerPoint® presentation or we can physically draw an umbrella on a blank sheet of paper, and name the top of the umbrella "Our Human Resources, Inc.", below that we write "Your Administrative and Human Resource Department".

The underside of the umbrella has <u>two labels on each side</u> separated by the umbrella handle.

Those labels are Human Resources and Benefits on one side, and then Payroll and Worker's Compensation on the other (see Figure 1 on the following pages).

The choice of whether to use a laptop presentation versus drawings would depend on the sophistication of the prospect, your relationship with that prospect, and the setting.

In most businesses, I have found the drawing to be less intimidating and more effective. Everything said must be conversational. It is a peer-to-peer sale.

The advantage of drawing is that it helps to create a mental Mind Map. (19) A Mind Map is a diagram used to represent words, ideas, tasks, or other items linked to and arranged around a central key word or idea. It helps create a conceptual understanding of your subject.

Mind Maps are used to generate, visualize, structure, and classify ideas, and as an aid in study, organization, problem solving, decision making, and writing — wonderful teaching aids.

Mind Maps (19) help keep the balance between mental significance and the real, palpable world.

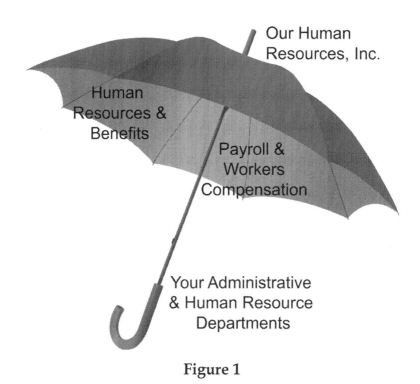

Figure 1

CHAPTER NINE: The Overview

<u>STEP 1</u>

Starting your conversation with the topic of Human Resources is a good idea because trends reported by Ernst & Young, SHRM, and Saratoga Institute indicate that most business owners are concerned about aspects of Human Resources dealing with:

Regulatory Compliance

Getting Paperwork Done On Time To

Avoid Penalties

Employee Handbooks

Job Descriptions

Affordable Care Act (ACA)

There are many other issues, but we are giving this 'Overview' for two purposes only.

1. To get our prospect in a 'HR Frame Of Mind'

2. As a Set Up For upcoming Commonality of Issues Sheet (7) (Step 2) –to find "PAIN" (Hot Buttons)! *Personal Inventory Assessment*

Preamble: Set an upfront agreement with the prospect in the first call that details your role and purpose while setting the agenda for the sales process and clarifying that *they will make the decision, and have the authority to do so.* Get clarity on the reasons they chose to talk with you. Make sure they have the money to invest in a solution (is your company profitable?), and that they are the only decision maker.

Example of Step 1: (Conversational)

"A good way to look at a Professional Employer Organization is with a simple drawing. We could actually name the top of this umbrella Risk Avoidance, Inc. (say this as you write the name "Our Human Resources, Inc." (Your actual company name), because that is what Professional Employer Organizations do—*overall risk avoidance* of these points— Human Resource Compliance, Benefits, Payroll and Workers' Compensation."

"Under the Human Resource part here, we provide the infrastructure to handle regulatory compliance issues, provide employee handbooks and help with job descriptions; we do the paperwork so your company can pick up their productivity. Plus, you have consultations by a human resource professional, or safety personnel as needed."

"On the Benefits side, we have relationships with major carriers, so we can administer health benefit plans and supplemental insurances; or do the administration for your current policies."

"Payroll is done utilizing cutting edge technology-software, and the right people with years of experience and multi-state experience."

"Under Workers' Compensation, we have several plans to help you gain control of this potential risk to your bottom line."

"We are a giant resource for our clients, and are available when called on, but are never intrusive."

Each one of the above points can, and should be extrapolated on and fully explained.

CHAPTER TEN: The Commonality of Issues Sheet (CIS)

Personal Inventory Assessment

STEP 2

(Memorize this — or read it to prospect)

"Let's take a closer look at your company (Prospect Name), and see if there is a potential fit."

"Over the years that we've been in business we have seen a commonality of issues that most business owners have regarding what we do. Please take a moment and fill this out."

"It also has the added benefit of letting us both know if I can be of any help. If I can't be, I'll leave."

Once you have done the Commonality of Issues Sheet, you will have the point specific issues that interest the CEO — their "hot buttons" i.e., their "pains". **Only** discuss these issues that are real to them, the ones that they have indicated. Remember this CIS is a compilation of what previous PEO buyers had as hot buttons.

Yes, there are many bells and whistles that are offered in PEO, and the thought running through our minds is — "Just wait until s/he sees____, (not on the list) s/he will really want our services."

While not appearing logical anything you say on any issue that is not checked as "Needs Improvement" on the Commonality of Issues Sheet can open Pandora's Box and impede your sale.

Many of the services offered are things many CEOs have only dreamt about, and we do not want them getting into a major study on the PEO offering, we want them as clients — NOW! Our offering is not rocket-science let's not turn it into it. Stay on the same *reality* page with the prospect CEO, do the process.

In my PEO industry experience, I have seen countless Human Resource Analysis sheets to determine needs. Most of them are excellent.

Most range from a two-page document to a six-page document. Why not use one of those? They certainly are much more intricate.

The answer is that in sales they would be a violation of the "Vital Few and the Useful Many" principle. The *Personal Inventory Assessment/* CIS Sheet is the "Vital Few".

We are only mining for the 'Vital Few' that were part of the Perfect Client Profile, the psychographics and the surveys. Anything else would be classified as the "Useful (or trivial) Many".

The Commonality of Issues Sheet (CIS) is compiled from surveys that were done on the PEO Perfect Client Profile club.

These are the clients that are currently utilizing PEO services, and they were kind enough to share their reasons for buying — their hot buttons.

The Human Resource Analysis that is six-pages long is an excellent tool *after the sale*, but not in making the sale.

Remember, sell them what they "want" — deliver what they want and need." (2)

Our Human Resources, Inc.

(A Professional Employer Organization)

COMMONALITY OF ISSUES

MOST BUSINESS OWNERS-CEO'S EXPERIENCE

Do you have an issue with?

(**www.rapidsalessuccess.com** for a copy under RSS TOOLS.)

(Needs Improvement? / In Control?)

1. Cost of Employees dollars lost from the bottom line?

2. Payroll... Job costing, timely, effective, accurate?

3. Are lawsuits or disputes very close to becoming frustrating and expensive, even when you are right?

4. Customer Retention... impact to your bottom line?

5. Audits: OSHA, DOL, Worker Comp, State Unemployment?

6. 401(k)?

7. Government Regulations: HR is in full legal compliance?

8. Worker Comp modifier going up or down?

9. Terminations... legal consequences?

10. Benefits... too costly- time spent answering questions?

11. Vision... does anyone share or participate in yours?

12. HR Department... a profit center?

13. Employee Retention (working for your competitor?)

14. Does company implement change easily?

CHAPTER ELEVEN: Radical Recall System

<u>STEP 3</u>

The Radical Recall System is designed to get our Owner-CEO into any past **issues** that may have affected cash flow, the company, and/or them personally, as regards PEO services. This process presents the paradigm shift from sales to consultant. It must be done precisely.

Why do this? To show the prospect that things can go wrong, and it hurts, and then to show them, (down the road) that we might have prevented it or lessened the damage.

<u>PEO is an emotional purchase, be empathetic</u>, or you will lose. The PEO buyer, in order to justify the emotional purchase decision, uses logic.

The steps in the (Radical) Rapid Recall System: (Memorize this)

    1. "Tell me about that (issue from the CIS that they said "Needs Improvement.)"

    2. "When did that happen?"

    3. "What did that cost you?"

4. "How did that affect your business?"

5. "How did that affect you, personally?" and "What impact?"

6. "On a scale of 1 to 10 how committed are you to fixing that?"

7. "What would make it a 10?"

8. If you cannot get it to a "10" ask, "Is there an earlier time this same sort of thing happened?"

If there is, go back to Step 1 and repeat all on the newly found item. If no, re-investigate each pain given.

It is important to get all of the answers on each question (you may have to probe, while still being conversational). What you are looking for is the emotional response, and the commitment of a "10" to fixing it.

The idea here, after getting a "10", is to move to the next item checked off in the "Needs Improvement" area of the Commonality of Issues Sheet (CIS) — The more the better.

There are statistics that show if you get multiple different Issues, your closing percentages skyrocket to well over 50%. **DO NOT PRESENT SOLUTIONS AT THIS STAGE** even though it is tempting. Have courage and follow the process.

We know that most business owners are skeptical of change. Not just a little bit, but a lot. They have fought long and hard to be where they are, and so are extremely hesitant to change anything. And, we all know that change is painful.

Many times that is because change represents introducing a more orderly method, and the rule here is that anytime you introduce order, you always get confusion. In fact, if you are experiencing confusion, find what order is being introduced. I keep repeating this because it is so important.

Confusion is handled by continuing to introduce order — do not chase the confusion — it is a red herring. A red herring is any diversion intended to distract attention from the main issue.

All of us, including the business owner, operate on what appears to be a linear time track and what <u>was</u> painful moments ago, quickly steps into the past, and then the distant past. We forget — easily.

A lot of Type "A" or "ADD" personalities have a tendency to dash in euphorically, and attack the next situation or project. We seem to enjoy putting out those fires.

The emotions and pains that we felt just moments, or a few days/months before, are forgotten. The RSS data has a system for correcting most of that with the Rapid Recall System.

Pain has to overwhelm the dislike of change in a prospect for them to act. _The pain creates a necessity for action, a demand for change._

This area requires training and role-playing to get it right.

Read it. Role-play it. Do it.

CHAPTER TWELVE: Gathering Data

STEP 4

When data gathering, have a sheet pre-prepared that shows exactly what you need to do a Request For Proposal (RFP). When gathering data, have a sheet pre-prepared that shows exactly what you need to do a Request For Proposal (RFP)- gotcha again. Asking for this information should be nonchalant, AND <u>matter of fact</u>.

<u>This step of the sale threatens your entire future client relationship</u>. It really does, and yet it seems so boring. The Prospect is filled with enthusiasm and everything "feels" okay. However, It must be done smoothly and expeditiously, with minimal effort on the prospects part or there could be troubled waters ahead.

They forget your sales interview just like they forget past pain.

Many sales have gone south because we can't get the paperwork out of the prospect. This is generally caused by not moving quickly enough after you have built up the heat, or asking them to FAX something to you. Avoid this. Prospects do not do homework, normally.

Often the CEO or Owner does not have a clue about a workers' compensation file or a state unemployment file, etc. What they do know is their business and their core competencies. We must find who works these programs/files and go directly to them *with the CEO, if possible*, to get paperwork necessary, in order to intelligently and profitably make a proposal.

Even better let the CEO know you will need these things at your first meeting when setting up your First Call. Fax them your list.

Ask them as you walk through the door if they have the data you requested. Try and make them produce it right now. **This is a critical area.**

CHAPTER THIRTEEN: Custom Presentation

Step 5

After doing the following:

The Overview of the PEO Industry

The Commonality of Issues Sheet

The (Radical) Rapid Recall System

The Gathering of Data

You are ready for a presentation that will have significant psychological impact on your prospect

Now, you can take what you know about the areas checked off as "Needs Improvement" on the CIS and be wonderfully creative. The process is all about their issues, their business, and, most importantly, *at their reality level.*

Depending on time and complexity, this could mean a second call. It is important at this solutions presentation, if it is a second call, to *have an agenda and make it known to the prospect*.

Example Agenda (7)

1. Recap of last meeting/or what we just talked about (Commonality of Issues) <u>Go through each issue</u>, as a reminder.

2. Presentation-addressing the solutions.

3. Presentation of Numbers.

You must have a thorough understanding of all numbers and should be able to communicate them smoothly.

Remember that the structure of these steps (the right steps in the right order) provides the psychological impact.

This process also makes the prospect aware that they are getting a point specific diagnosis for their situations. It does not 'feel' like a one size fits all solution.

CHAPTER FOURTEEN: The Cost Box

STEP 6

Why do we fear pricing? Why is it that this one aspect is so overwhelming?

Because it is true — it is scary, and it is a bit overwhelming, but only if you have not done value added, pain-based selling. You obviously have to know the numbers cold. Many times, part of that fear we feel is that we need more comfort with the numbers ourselves.

What is value-added selling? (New Definition)

*It is selling according to the prospect's perceived needs (see: wants, as perceived needs are "wants"). That IS what **they** value.*

It is discovering through this Radical PEO Sales system those things that the prospect perceives as real and then coming up with solutions (value) to address those point specific concerns, only.

Your typical client __NEEDS__ what you sell, and your Perfect Client __WANTS__ what you sell. (2)

If we have done each step of the Rapid Recall System to completion, we are telling the prospect the price of something they have already bought in their mind. We do not need to be concerned with endless cost justification comparison and lengthy spreadsheets.

Yes, we should have all of that available, but be hesitant to use it. Numbers do not sell PEO products and services; emotions and *Personal Inventory Assessment Selling* do.

Note that numbers can also act as a misunderstood symbol so let your prospect be the guide, don't just dive in. You can also reduce PEO numbers to an hourly or daily level and use, e.g., it's not $1000 per year, and it is $2.74 per day.

In regard to PEO, the services offered are already in our prospect's budget. What they already have set aside for, or accidentally spend on employee administration is being spent now. We simply do the same things, but with no hassle, and an expertise they could not possibly afford.

They normally do not have the enriched services that PEO brings to the table and they <u>do</u> <u>not</u> <u>have</u> <u>the</u> <u>expertise</u>, or they are spending a lot of time and money on administration unnecessarily.

> There is software for an "Administrative Cost Justification/Analysis". Email me at jc@rapidsalessuccess.com and I'll will send it to you, or visit the website at www.rapidsalessuccess.com - It is under "RSS Tools". You will have questions on this, and those questions will be answered for you. Once thoroughly learned it is a wonderful tool.

There is no escaping the numbers. You might as well get comfortable with them.

In some circumstances, the prospect is not spending enough money on their employees. In this instance, PEO services can be easy to sell if the prospect is profitable, and <u>if</u> they consider their own time valuable, as they will have experienced a lot of turnover.

Turnover cost money. The costs are estimated to be 2½ to 4 times annual salary. We have a worksheet, entitled "Ghosts" to determine that cost also (See the website). The cost is inordinate. Money that our prospect CEOs think they are saving by doing it all themselves is lost in one or two unnecessary terminations of key employees.

In the first call we should understand that this business is not a dollar-qualified prospect yet. They are only qualified from a Perfect Client Profile perspective. A dollar-qualified prospect is one that is profitable and generally expanding. We are finding out this information as we do the first call. It is okay to ask, "Is your company profitable yet?" Be sure and congratulate them if they are.

When we look, a PEO's ability to deliver:

- Regulatory compliance
- Payroll,
- 401(k),
- Medical plans,
- Plans administration,
- Dental,
- Vision,
- Human resource consulting,
- Better cash flow,
- Predictability of employee costs

And the list goes on…

There is not a bigger bargain on the planet. Plus, the client and their staff are now focused on their core competencies and driving more dollars to the bottom line.

CHAPTER FIFTEEN: Handling Objections

STEP 7

We should become adept at handling clients' objections. We should appear calm, cool and collected on the outside, when sometimes the exact opposite is true on the inside.

We have to be actors.

"All the world's a stage,
and all the men and women merely players;
they have their exits and their entrances,
and one man in his time plays many parts..."
~William Shakespeare

Or, try this — really. Tell the prospect that you are terrible at handling objections and ask if they will help you work through this phase. You cannot be smiling when you say this. This can have a profound and positive effect. Get ready for the paradigm shift of a prospect becoming a partner and teacher, alongside of you.

If you do an Internet search for handling objections you would discover 52,000+ articles. Amazing! *I am saying if you concentrate on handling objections you will get them.*

There is **ALWAYS** a handful of what I call silent objections in the PEO sale.

1. Loyalty (of prospect's employees)

2. Control (fear of CEO losing control of this side of the business)

3. Cost (most buyers will challenge cost, even if they think it is fair

4. Corporate Culture (a huge, generally unrecognized area that is overlooked)

All buyers will have these objections—It is part of the game. Buyers are expected to have objections. Most objections are not serious—not if you have precisely followed the process.

Let's take the usual objections one at a time.

1. Loyalty—The CEO is fearful that employees will start being loyal to us, instead of them. This comes about from not fully understanding the off-site nature of PEO, and not fully understanding the co-employment relationship.

Answering the Objection: "Jeremy, everyone entering into this arrangement has that same question—and let me say, "We are the *co-employer of record for* **administrative purposes only**.

"Employees normally look at this as a smart decision on your part, as it is explained in our orientation, that you hired us to do the paperwork. Employees also see that you are trying to make their lives better."

2. Control—The Owner/CEO feels she will lose control of her employees. The fear may exist, but fortunately this objection is not reality.

Answering Objection: "Christine, the only control question is one regarding gain. You have gained control of your costs and found someone else to do the paperwork, and you will spend more time with your employees because of it. Furthermore, our agreement gives you the right to terminate our services. You're the boss." A PEO relationship allows them to gain more control.

3. Cost—if we have done our job on the pain-based selling side or not, this always comes up. They want the pricing explained, but they really have few concerns about the price, if you are priced fairly. We have a software tool that will help the Prospect CEO understand what they are spending now—<u>most do not know</u>, as they do not have a precise definition of "payroll burden" (see definition in glossary) and all that is involved in it. *This is important.*

Answering the Objection: The truth is PEO services are very inexpensive. To prove this, look in your local newspaper or business journal for those companies declaring bankruptcy, and then research it a little to discover the reasons why.

Call up one of those owners and talk to them and find out, or call your CPA and ask her.

What you will find is that they could not pay their taxes (940-941), they could not find and keep good employees, they had fines and penalties that drove them out of business, or they had massive cash flow issues (Department of Labor audits, Worker's Compensation audits), or regulatory issues. These are the solutions you bring to the table — PEOs <u>are a bargain</u>. Also, if the prospect tried to build on their own what I can give them for pennies on the dollar, they couldn't come anywhere near the scope and depth of what I can provide for the price being charged.

Another question to ask is… "How much money did you spend on office supplies last year?" Then I ask them the same question about how much they spent on their employees. More times than not, they spent more money on office supplies, and it becomes much easier to discuss the problems with how they are spending money in addition to the opportunity cost of not investing more money on their employees. Sometimes, they even start to laugh because they quickly see the insanity of it. (I stole this from a Peak Performer). (18)

4.Corporate Culture — This issue is when a company, generally 30+ employees, has been working hard at selling their own employees on what they do, and how good they are. It is a form of "internal branding of corporate identity". When they start asking questions on corporate culture you have, generally, already lost the battle. **It should have been mentioned in the overview or more appropriately in the presentation.**

Answering the Objection: You, the consultant, should give this as one of your company's objection-EARLY.

Okay, if you are not used to it, it can be a little daunting.

Client says, "You know, everything is looking good."

You say, (gulp) "That's great Conor, but I still have a few concerns."

Conor says, (mildly shocked) "What are they?"

You say, *"My company is always concerned about the corporate culture of our new clients that we bring on, we want to make sure that the CEOs of our client companies have a getting better agenda and know that it is their employees who will help get them there. We want to work with like-minded companies."* (22)

This is also the time to bring up loyalty and control if they have not already done so. **Loyalty and control are objections that are always there in the PEO world**, but rarely voiced.

You might as well get it on the table. You do not want a sale to blow up at the last minute with an unexpressed objection. PEOs are looking for long-term relationships, not the quick sale that will be here today, but gone tomorrow. You should be too. Can you say claw back?

NEGATIVE – REVERSE OBJECTION HANDLING WORKS

(Do this before you close, particularly if prospect is not raising objections).

"Brigid (Business Owner), I have a few concerns that I would like to address." Then you unload, one at a time, every objection you can think of that they might have, and let them handle it.

It is fun and effective — try it. It is another paradigm shift.

CHAPTER SIXTEEN: The Close

STEP 8 (The Questions)

When would you like your first payroll?

We will need to set up an orientation meeting to get you started by the first of the month.

It sounds like we have a new client, thank you.

When would you like your first payroll to begin?

What would you like me to do next? (A favorite of Peak Performers)

If the **Radical PEO Sales** process is followed you will find that some of your prospects are literally *buying* from you and closing themselves.

If the prospect is stuck on what to say for a closing statement I have found that saying, *"What would you like me to do next?"* gets them unstuck.

CHAPTER SEVENTEEN: Timeline for Implementing

STEP 9

The new client must have an understanding about what happens next. This could be called a future reality factor or, the steps on what happens next.

If the prospect gets confused or loses their excitement, they might stop the sale (not make a payroll). This also partially addresses "fear of change".

THIS IS IMPORTANT. A Client Calendar must be available, and explained step-by-step, showing them dates on what they have just purchased will be implemented. It gives them a secure feeling on the decision to be a client.

It is easy to print a blank calendar and fill in what date you need:

- Employee email addresses
- Employee proof of citizenship
- Medical Health Documents
- Date for formal Orientation

- The Implementation date on the handling of your new client's original pain. Etcetera.

CHAPTER EIGHTEEN: Referrals

<u>STEP 10</u>

There is a close relationship between the items checked as "Need Improvement" on the Commonality of Issues Sheet and the sale of PEO services. The prospect is checking off which items are her/his hot buttons/pains.

Earlier I stated that we should sell prospects what they want, but deliver what they want and need.

The reason is clear; people always buy what they want. A want is merely a perceived need. Your typical prospect **NEEDS** what you sell, but your <u>ideal prospect</u> **WANTS** what you sell, remember?

As your prospects transition to a new client status and move into the on-boarding process of orientation and first payroll, you have the ability to truly impact this new client and cement your relationship by delivering, as closely to instant as is possible, those items they wanted — the items they checked off on the Commonality of Issues Sheet.

This attention and support to the new client, easing any possible concerns, will make your services that much more valuable to them, and prevent buyer's remorse.

In fact, as a consultative professional you should always make sure that what you have promised is delivered. Let the client know that you are their advocate. This goes a long way in getting healthy referrals.

The top 20% always ask for referrals and keep getting them.

EFFECTIVE PRESENTATIONS

Think about it: Your **R**equest **F**or **P**roposal volume is in the basement, sales are dropping, and you're dreading the weekly meeting with your sales manager or owner, when suddenly a prospect you've been after calls and wants to see you.

When the euphoria dies down (almost instantly), you realize that the fate of this sale rests in your hands and you're not 100% sure you're up to it! You really need the sale and you don't want to blow this.

Be prepared for every presentation. When the economy slips, the little things become more important than ever.

You should always be prepared to make a presentation. Make sure you complete your research on this possible new client well in advance of any presentation so you'll know exactly what to say, and when to say it. Do the Radical PEO Sales process by the numbers.

Knowledge is power only when acted upon, and you'll need all the power you can get to sell more, more often!

Utilize PowerPoint® presentations if applicable. It is one of the best tools you can use if the setting demands it. It is user-friendly and allows you to move through an entire presentation with accuracy, flexibility, speed, and persuasiveness. If not, use the Mind Map. (19)

Practice, practice, practice. Like any winning athlete practice each presentation and the steps in materials in advance to sharpen your message and close the sale.

Read it. Role-play it. Do it.

CHAPTER NINETEEN: From Confusion to Clarity

<u>Here is the Radical PEO Sales process at work once again</u>

Let's say average business owners work anywhere from 60-80 hours per week. Their schedules are horrendous. They are generally a Type A personality. Right now, they have a lot of worry over the economy, lines of credit and slumping sales.

They are typically married, love their families, have children and know that the business is what supports all of that plus their somewhat lavish lifestyle, e.g., house, cars, nanny (part-time), vacations, boat, summer property, camp for the kids, clothing.

Let's say also that <u>any person</u> has only 100 mental attention bits, kind of like RAM (random access memory) of availability to think and comprehend with.

Let us imagine now that this prospect has 60% of the those mental attention bits on his work (lots of issues, and that is kind of normal), 6% on being tired and/or hungry, and 14% on a sick youngster at home, and an additional 5% on making a 6:00 P.M. meeting, and being prepared. He is 85% occupied.

And now you, the <u>salesperson</u>, walk through his door for your 4:00 P.M. First Call. This gives you a 15% person to talk with, and you have not even said hello.

If you launch into a usual getting to know you rapport thing, which is generally a tell me about that (picture on your wall) line, and then a quick presentation highlighting the features, benefits and incentives of your company and its products, flashing a brochure or showing a PowerPoint presentation filled with acronyms and perhaps words that our business owner does not understand—well then, you are relying on two things only.

Number one, the prospect's good grace in just not falling to sleep, or worse—engaging themselves in what I call "objection mode"—just to stay awake, or, number two, he knows about the PEO industry and was hoping you'd show up—(pre-sold).

Now let's say you have the same circumstances but you walk in with the Rapid Sales Success process, as a <u>consultant</u>.

You introduce yourself and establish some rapport, hopefully about the thing he really loves — his business, and the next thing he knows you are sitting there making a drawing of some principle called Human Resource Outsourcing — what is that an umbrella?

Our Human Resources, Inc.

Human Resources & Benefits

Payroll & Workers Compensation

Your Administrative & Human Resource Departments

(This prospect is forced into the present by your actions of engagement.) He thinks, "Oh yeah, there's the umbrella handle and labels on each side of the handle — human resource, benefits and then payroll and worker's comp — hmm — so what — at least he's interesting".

Then he hears you say that—"most CEOs have some kind of commonality of issues", and the consultant shoves this form toward you and says something about—"if I am wasting your time, I'll leave"—(sounds good)—what's he talking about anyway?

Oh yeah, human resources and benefits and geez, worker's compensation stuff. Good Lord, he wants me to take a test. Oh well, let me at least look at it.

Hmm! (Prospect looking at CIS) we do need some improvement on this one, and this one too, what the heck, I guess it can't hurt to fill it out. He gives you the Commonality of Issues Sheet back.

Now you, _the consultant_, start taking each question that he said "Needs Improvement" on, and doing the Rapid Recall System showing a proper acknowledgement after each answer—having empathy.

You say, "Worker's Compensation" rates are going up?"

He says, "Yes they are…"

You say, "Ouch! Tell me about that."

He does.

Then you acknowledge what he just said and ask, "When was that?"

Prospect answers and you acknowledge. "Okay." Then, "What did _that_ cost you?"

Prospect answers and you ask, after a low whistle. "How did that affect your business?"

Prospect answers and you acknowledge and say, "And, how did that affect you personally?"

Prospect answers and you give an appropriate acknowledgement and ask, "What impact did that have?"

Prospect answers and you once again acknowledge his answer, and then say, "Okay, on a scale from one to ten how committed are you to fixing that?"

I promise you this guy is not going to fall to sleep or start in with any kind of "Objection Mode" thing—he is fully engaged now.

He is engaged because he is communicating on something that is important to him—his concerns, his worries, his business, his lifestyle, his wife, his kids, his boat. Please note also, HE is communicating. You are merely asking questions.

Let's say however that this prospect has the opposite reaction and will not even look at the umbrella and will not fill out the Commonality of Issues Sheet. What should you do?

Leave. Yes, leave. Do it nicely, but get out of there.

Why? Look, all kinds of current PEO clients that were eventually called "Perfect Clients" because they were so nice to work with ended up helping to formulate the "Perfect Client Profile" club, and this prospect just voted himself out of that exclusive club. He self-deselected. Next.

There could be a bunch of reasons he wouldn't play, and quite honestly, it is probably not important.

He just saved you from wasting a lot of time, effort, energy and money.

Okay, if you insist, put him on a drip marketing campaign and call him once more after a few weeks if you like.

CHAPTER TWENTY: Corporation You!

This chapter talks more about the concept of treating your sales career like your own business.

Let's clarify the concept by saying that if you believe the advantage of owning your own business is the freedom to play golf three times and week and take as many vacations a year as you want, we may have a problem.

Remember in Chapter Nineteen we talked about the typical business owner's profile. They work 60 to 80 hours per week, their schedules are horrendous, and they are generally a Type A personality. Also, in chapter 4 we talked about the 80-20 Rule, this same rule applies to successful sales professionals. If you want to be in that top 20% of successful sales professionals, you will need to put in a little extra time, you will need to plan your schedule, you will need to have a CRM tool that helps keep you organized and on target.

End your day updating your CRM with notes and to dos from your day, have tomorrow's schedule finalized in detail and ready to go.

Not only do you need to have a goal for your year, but also you need to know exactly where you are at with the goal.

As a business owner, you would be watching your results, as the owner of your career, manage your results. Not just your goals—look around and pay attention to the time wasters. I once pointed out to a sales rep that had been attending a weekly networking meeting that he mentioned he wasn't getting good results that he needed to consider the ROI on everything he did. His networking meetings was roughly an hour each Wednesday, he spend 15 minutes (at minimum) getting to the meeting, and another 15 minutes getting back to his office or to his next appointment. The lunch cost him around $8.00 with tip and he had been doing it for over a year. He had invested 78 hours, and over $416.00 dollars, and he had nothing to show for it.

Value your time, invest a couple extra hours each day, be organized, plan your days and you'll be one of the top producing 20% sales consultants in the PEO industry.

CHAPTER TWENTY-ONE: Learn to let go

If I see a common problem with sales people who aren't as successful as they could be in the PEO Industry it's learning when to let go. First of all, remember how we discussed your contact needs to be the business owner, don't fall into the trap of not adhering to this rule.

The only individual who has the ability to make the decision you need to have made is the business owner — period. Your first audience needs to be with the business owner, he may have you work with some of the staff members through the process, but unless you are in front of the owner you are not going to be successful the majority of the time.

Don't allow yourself to become a professional visitor. I've seen it over and over again, sales reps doing what I will refer to as a drive by. Hey I was in the neighborhood and I thought I'd stop by — Blah, Blah, Blah.
Wrap your mind around the fact that you are a professional, a consultant, and that you represent one of the finest Professional Employer Organizations in the Country. Your time has value. If you act like your time has no value than your prospects will treat you that way.

GLOSSARY

Control: The activity of managing something from start to finish.

Critical Success Factor (CSF): Is a business term for an element that is necessary for an organization or project to achieve its mission. They are the **critical factors** or activities required for ensuring the **success** of your business (Vital Few).

Consultant: an expert who gives advice.

Courage: A quality of spirit that enables you to face danger in spite of fear.

Fear: False Evidence Appearing Real — An emotion experienced in "anticipation" of some specific pain.

Influence: Shape or influence; give direction to.

Managing: Come to terms or deal successfully with.

Manipulate: Control (others or oneself), or influence skillfully.

Mind Map: A diagram used to represent words, ideas, tasks, arranged and linked to a central key idea.

Nomenclature: A system of words used to name things in a particular discipline.

Precise: Characterized by perfect conformity to fact or truth; strictly correct.

Psychographics: Complete psychological profile of an actual buyer.

Psychology: Is an academic and applied discipline involving the scientific study of mental functions, and behaviors.

Psychologists study such phenomena as perception, cognition, emotion, personality, behavior, and interpersonal relationships.

Psychology also refers to the application of such knowledge to various spheres of human activity, including issues related to everyday life.

Sales Demographics: *Physical* characteristics identifying a buyer for a particular industry.

Sales Psychologist: An applied discipline involving the scientific application of processes dealing with mental functions and behavior in a business environment. A Sales Psychologists determines if there should be an exchange of goods or services for an agreed sum of money.

Selling: The activity of persuading someone to buy.

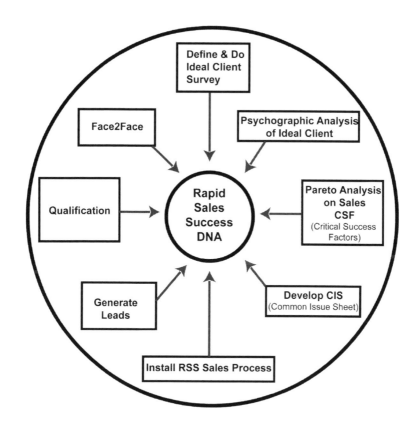

BIBLIOGRAPHY

And/Or Other Books Referenced or Recommended by This Author

1. American Management Association. Various Courses.

2. Assaraf, John; Smith, Murray, The Answer. May 20, 2008.

3. Bandler, Richard. *Frogs Into Princes. Neuro Linguistic Programming.* Feb 1979.

4. Collins, Jim, "Good to Great: Why Some Companies Make the Leap... and Others Don't, ©2001, HarperCollins Publishers, Inc., New York.

5. Critical Success Factors: D. Ronald Daniel of McKinsey & Company developed the concept of "success factors" in 1961. The process was refined by Jack F. Rockart, of MIT's Sloan School of Management in 1986. In 1995 James A. Johnson and Michael Friesen applied it to many sector settings, including health care.

6. Daniel, D. Ronald, "Management Information Crisis," Harvard Business Review, September-October, 1961, p. 111.

7. Duncan, Garry. Leadership Connections 1998 – 2000.

8. Ernst & Young http://www.ey.com/ - One of the world's leading professional services organizations, helps companies across the globe to identify and capitalize on business opportunities.

9. Family Education Network.

10. Freese, Thomas A., "Secrets of Question Based Selling: How the Most Powerful Tool in Business Can Double Your Sales Results," Published by Sourcebooks, Inc., 2000.

11. Gladwell, Malcolm. "Blink." April 3, 2007.

12. Grinder, John. "Frogs Into Princes - Neuro Linguistic Programming." Feb 1979.

13. Jantsch, John. "Duct Tape Marketing." May 13, 2008.

14. "Joseph Juran, 103, Pioneer in Quality Control, Dies" by Nick Bunkley, The New York Times, Obituary, March 3, 2008.

15. Juran, Joseph and Godfrey, A. Blanton, "Juran's Quality Control Handbook," Sections 5.24 (Vital Few and Useful Many) and 8.20 (Pareto Diagram), 5th Edition, ©1998 by McGraw-Hill, Inc.

16. Kennedy, Dan 2006, No B.S. Direct Marketing, Direct Marketing For Non-Direct Marketing Businesses, Entrepreneur Press.

17. Maltz, Maxwell. "Psycho–Cybernetics." Aug 15, 1989.

18. Mangini, Tom. San Francisco, CA (quoted from a personal email in 2009).

19. "Mind Maps" is claimed as a trademark by The Buzan Organisation, Ltd. in the UK and the USA. The trade-mark does not appear in the records of the Canadian Intellectual Property Office. In the U.S. "Mind Maps" is trademarked as a "service mark" for "EDUCATIONAL SERVICES, NAMELY, CONDUCTING COURSES IN SELF-IMPROVEMENT."

20. NAPEO website, www.napeo.org.

21. Saratoga Institute
http://www.pwc.com/extweb/service.nsf/docid/de40ffb0d409
81d385256f17005397cd Saratoga, formerly EP-First & Saratoga,
is a global leader in the measurement and benchmarking of
human capital.

22. Sarvadi, Paul CEO/Founder – Administaff.

23. Professional Selling Skills System™, by Achieve Global™.

24. Shakespeare, William, "As You Like It," ©1997 by The
Folger Shakespeare Library. Washington Square Press, New
York, NY.

25. SHRM - Society for Human Resource Management –
Advances the human resource profession to ensure that HR is
recognized as an essential partner in developing and
executing organizational strategy.

26. Six Sigma is a registered service mark and trademark of
Motorola, Inc. via Motorola University.

WHAT OTHERS HAVE SAID...

"This is easy. Good golly, I was trying to kill a fly with a canon. This is the ultimate in relationship selling, because I am talking about this guy's business and the problems he is stuck in. My prospects love it. I used to just jabber now I have a system. Thanks!"
JA Los Angeles

"I just wanted to let you know that since I have been using the Rapid Sales Success Script my first calls are going much better. I am finding when either the prospect or I get off track this system gets me back to the subject. Being able to stay on track has proven most effective. I am able to cover more information, get a better conversation with my prospect and receive more valuable information from them."
SF Chicago

"Thank you for giving me the opportunity to read your new book. It's a home run in my opinion! I agree with 99% of what you say, and I've used much of what you discuss in teaching, training and selling myself. You've taken pages of "stuff" I have and made it short and sweet, easy to understand and easy to implement. Great job!"
TM San Francisco

"Joe is one of the greatest minds to the PEO and HRO industry. His approach to sales in "Rapid Sales Success" is by far the most effective and well-written training tools that I have ever come across. He has a website to accompany the book that provides tools to reinforce his book's techniques. His coaching demeanor is extraordinary and he takes a vested interest in your success. I highly recommend Joe and his book to anyone that is looking to have an advantage on their competition." ~BF

"Having been in sales for over 30 years, we finally get real insight into the Buyer's mindset and what REALLY goes right AND wrong in those sales calls. Do not miss another opportunity to close that sale and have a real client for life!" ~DL
"A must read! This is easily the best psychology on making a sale I have ever read. Love the focus, specific understanding of the sales game, and the winning strategy provided. Thanks for a superb read." ~JH

"Authentic, different and unique. I have read and now have put into practice these NEW principles and I am have a blast and more SUCCESS.
Thanks." ~MTJ.

ABOUT THE AUTHORS

About Rodney Diekema:

Rodney Diekema has spent over 20 years becoming one of the nation's leading "Employment Process Experts." Since 1992, Rod has been involved in the PEO "Professional Employer Organization" Industry. PEO's are simply a better way to manage employment. Having worked for 2 of the nation's largest PEO's, in 2007, he started his own PEO. In 2012, he decided to purchase PEO Network, and to focus on helping other PEO owners and startup PEOs grow the industry.

In December of 2012, Rodney Diekema hit five separate Amazon.com best-seller lists with "The Secret to Winning Big" book. Diekema has joined a select group of the world's leading experts, along with noted business development expert, best-selling author and speaker, Brian Tracy, to co-write the book titled, "The Secret to Winning Big: The World's Leading Experts Reveal Their Strategies for Winning Big In Life and Business." CelebrityPress—a leading business book publisher, released the book.

About Joe Caulfield

Joe Caulfield began his career in PEO in 1994. He watched as his new hire group tried, but largely failed at making the PEO sale. Within that first group, there was a 62% failure rate. This incident became his quest in discovering a PEO sales system that worked.

His breakthrough, showing that a prospect's present-time decisions are often filtered through a prism of past anxieties was groundbreaking – this is what left prospects with hesitancy and procrastination on buying decisions. It is also when you see the phenomena of a prospect tracking perfectly, but then NOT purchasing.

His books and coaching have specific tools, and processes that PEO sales consultants use to shine the spotlight of the prospect's critical thinking skills on any past anxieties, thereby allowing them to re-look at those areas with fresh eyes – quickly, and make a decision.

Joe firmly believes that our freedom to make correct decisions depend on the ability to alter our past conclusions, and that if we cannot change our mind; we become fixed and enslaved among barriers of our own creation.

31860121R00068

Made in the USA
Lexington, KY
28 April 2014